W9-BVD-440

SOCIAL LIVES OF
DOLPHINS

Sue LaNeve

Rourke
Educational Media

rourkeeducationalmedia.com

*Scan for Related Titles
and Teacher Resources*

Teaching Focus:
Phonemic Awareness: Alliteration. Have students find words with the same beginning sounds.

Before Reading:

Building Academic Vocabulary and Background Knowledge
Before reading a book, it is important to set the stage for your child or student by using pre-reading strategies. This will help them develop their vocabulary, increase their reading comprehension, and make connections across the curriculum.

1. Read the title and look at the cover. *Let's make predictions about what this book will be about.*
2. Take a picture walk by talking about the pictures/photographs in the book. Implant the vocabulary as you take the picture walk. Be sure to talk about the text features such as headings, Table of Contents, glossary, bolded words, captions, charts/diagrams, and Index.
3. Have students read the first page of text with you then have students read the remaining text.
4. Strategy Talk – use to assist students while reading.
   - Get your mouth ready
   - Look at the picture
   - Think…does it make sense
   - Think…does it look right
   - Think…does it sound right
   - Chunk it – by looking for a part you know
5. Read it again.
6. After reading the book complete the activities below.

Content Area Vocabulary
Use glossary words in a sentence.

affectionate
distressed
nurture
self-aware
sociable
wake

After Reading:

Comprehension and Extension Activity
After reading the book, work on the following questions with your child or students in order to check their level of reading comprehension and content mastery.

1. *What is a group of dolphins called?* (Asking questions)
2. *What types of dolphins does a pod contain?* (Summarize)
3. *What does a mother do immediately after a calf is born?* (Text to self connection)
4. *After reading the book, what can you summarize about dolphins?* (Summarize)

Extension Activity
Dolphins are faced with many dangers as they try and thrive in their ocean habitat. There are things you can do to make people more aware of this. If you enjoy performing, why not get together with some friends and put on a dolphin play or concert at your school to raise awareness of some of the dangers they face? If your school puts on a special play or assembly each year maybe you could suggest an underwater theme.

TABLE OF CONTENTS

DYNAMIC DOLPHINS

In the sparkling ocean waters, bottlenose dolphins surface and swim alongside a sailboat.

One rolls in a somersault. Another leaps through the air, then splashes

into the sea. Two more race in the **wake** of the boat's bow.

Dolphins are mammals, not fish. They can hold their breath for seven minutes, but must surface to breathe.

These **sociable** mammals like each other's company. A group of dolphins is called a pod. Each pod contains two to 40 dolphins. A pod might contain female cows and their calves, a group of male bulls and male calves, or perhaps a cow and bull.

Sometimes a pod includes hundreds of dolphins of different colors and species. If you see a single dolphin, it is usually a bull.

Affectionate dolphins enjoy touching each other. When a dolphin rests a pectoral fin on another dolphin, it may mean they are friends.

Mother cows **nurture** their calves. A newborn calf must breathe immediately, so the mother guides it to the surface.

DOLPHIN TALK

Dolphins are chatty mammals. They communicate with whistles, clicks, and squeals. Their signature whistles help them identify each other.

They make clicking sounds to search for food and track enemies.

Using echolocation, dolphins emit clicks that bounce off fish or other objects. The echo gives the dolphin information about the object's size, shape, and location.

Like people, dolphins feel stress and fear. When a dolphin gets in trouble, it calls for help with a distinctive whistle.

CARING CREATURES

Dolphins care about each other. A pod will work together to save a **distressed** member.

Dolphins are sensitive to pain and stress. Their limbic system—the brain area that handles emotions—is larger than ours!

Dolphins feel sadness. When a calf dies, a mother cow may swim slowly and not eat.

They feel joy, too. Dolphins will blow a bubble through their blowholes and play with it. When they receive a treat, they often squeal with glee.

Rare albino dolphins turn pink when they are angry, sad, or embarrassed.

Their thin skin shows the blood vessels underneath. Like people, these dolphins blush!

SMART AND SPLASHY

Dolphins are smart! They like to play with people. Their large brains make it easy for them to learn tricks and imitate their trainers.

They are also **self-aware** and enjoy looking at themselves in a mirror.

Most sea creatures must constantly search for food. Echolocation lets dolphins find food quickly, giving them more time for play.

Dolphins behave like people in many ways. They enjoy company, and they love to play. They feel stress and sadness. They also protect each other and nurture their young.

So why do dolphins swim in a boat's wake? Is it to speed their journey? To race? Or just for fun? What do you think?

PHOTO GLOSSARY

affectionate (uh-FEK-shuh-nit): Showing or feeling a tenderness, fondness, or love.

distressed (di-STRES-t): To suffer or show extreme emotional pain or unhappiness.

nurture (NUR-chur): To care for, protect, and encourage the growth of something or someone.

self-aware (self-uh-WAIR): The ability to see oneself as different from others.

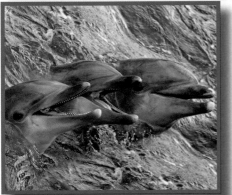

sociable (SOH-shuh-buhl): One who is friendly and enjoys the company of others.

wake (wayk): The trail of water that rushes downstream as a boat moves forward.

INDEX

WEBSITES TO VISIT

www.animalfactguide.com/animal-facts/
  bottlenose-dolphin
www.earthintransition.org/2010/06/theyre-
  super-brainy-too
www.dolphinsmart.org/dsrefreshertraining/
  index.php/main/nav/17#1

Meet The Author!
www.meetREMauthors.com

ABOUT THE AUTHOR

The only thing Ms. LaNeve likes more than writing children's books is living aboard her trawler, *m/v Freebird*, cruising the ocean, and watching dolphins swim alongside. She holds an MFA from The Vermont College of Fine Arts and is a Merchant Marine Captain. She believes dolphins are magical.

Library of Congress PCN Data

Social Lives of Dolphins/ Sue LaNeve
(Animal Behaviors)
ISBN 978-1-68191-700-9 (hard cover)
ISBN 978-1-68191-801-3 (soft cover)
ISBN 978-1-68191-898-3 (e-Book)
Library of Congress Control Number: 2016932576

Rourke Educational Media
Printed in the United States of America, North Mankato, Minnesota

Also Available as:
ROURKE'S
e-Books

© 2017 Rourke Educational Media

www.rourkeeducationalmedia.com

PHOTO CREDITS: Cover © Willyam Bradberry Page 4-5 © Willyam Bradberry, Jeff Kinsey; Page 6-7 © Joost van Uffelen; Page 8-9 © eZeePics, vkilikov; Page 10-11 © KateChris, Willyam Bradberry; Page 12-13 © litvis, Matt9122; Page 14-15 © Willyam Bradberry, Sheldon Gardner, Christian Musat; Page 16-17 © Anirut Krisanakul; Page 18-19 © ChameleonsEye / Shutterstock.com, Lars Christensen / Shutterstock.com; Page 20-21 © Four Oaks, Jose Lledo; page 22 middle © Sergey Uryadnikov; dolphin tail logo © alexandrovskyi. All images from Shutterstock.com

Edited by: Keli Sipperley
Cover design, interior design and art direction: Nicola Stratford
www.nicolastratford.com